Witch. Bitch. Heretic.

Witch. Bitch. Heretic.

Prophecy, Poetry, and Prayer from the Soul of a Mom and Mystic

BY
Rebekah L. Solar

RESOURCE *Publications* · Eugene, Oregon

WITCH. BITCH. HERETIC.
Prophecy, Poetry, and Prayer from the Soul of a Mom and Mystic

Resource Publications
An Imprint of Wipf and Stock Publishers
199 W. 8th Ave., Suite 3
Eugene, OR 97401

www.wipfandstock.com

PAPERBACK ISBN: 979-8-3852-5322-7
HARDCOVER ISBN: 979-8-3852-5323-4
EBOOK ISBN: 979-8-3852-5324-1

VERSION NUMBER 11/24/25

To all those compassionately subversive misfits living authentically into your calling each day, know that this labor of love is for you. Your power, your presence, and your ministry have sustained me.

To the Holy Hooligans, you bring me such joy!

Contents

CONTENTS

CONTENTS

New Faith: You are Changed-Stuff

Letter To The Badasses

Beloved,

I do not want anything from you. I know things are really hard right now. Here too. New ways of doing ministry, less support, and routines being upended have become a new baseline for many of us. Hours of Zoom, Facebook Live, and video editing software are flooding our brains with blue light and draining our energy. Lack of useful resources and full voicemail boxes are regular stumbling blocks these days. This is hard! You are seen. Things are tough right now, but so are you! The demands on your time and energy are so high. Navigating this new world while caring for children, partners, parents . . . making sure there is enough clean laundry for today . . . I see you. You are gifted and called by God to love and serve God's people. The feelings you are having right now are valid. In those moments of deep and profound joy, those moments of sheer terror, and those moments when you want to strangle the people you live with . . . You may find you are feeling things in a more extreme fashion lately, laughing loudly and crying at the drop of a hat. Inversely, you may find yourself being numb or stuck in a funk or washed over by a general depression. You may go back and forth between these feelings. Try not to place judgement on your emotions. Allow yourself to feel them, as they are. It is okay to feel however you are feeling. It is also okay to seek out additional support. In fact, I highly encourage you to find a trusted friend you can share with or a counselor/therapist.

Your mental health is important to your overall health, and you are important to me, so take care of yourself!

I just wanted to let you know how much I love you, how amazing and fierce you are! It is your prayers, support, and encouragement that keep me going every day . . . especially on the days I would rather disappear to Greece and live on a boat. You demonstrate for me each day the power of the Holy Spirit and I am empowered to keep seeking Holy Wisdom through your example. Thank you for being you. Thank you for answering God's call. Thank you for showing the world new ways to love. I give thanks to God each day that They sent me such a circle of badasses with which to surround myself.

—Bekah

Creation: You are Earth-Stuff

Coming From Silence—Retreat Worship
On Genesis 1:1–3

(Enter in silence)

Take a deep breath in . . . and out.

As you breathe in, imagine the Spirit breathing life into you. As you breathe out, experience the release of your exhale, and allow your body to surrender more fully into the present moment. Continue to pay attention to your breath for a few cycles and then allow your breath to carry your awareness from your head down into your heart . . .

Prayer

Holy Spirit, Breath of God . . .

> For this breath, we thank you.
>
> For this breath, we love you.
>
> With this breath, we know you.
>
> With this breath, we share you.
>
> In this breath, we are filled with your presence,
> peace, and power.

I invite you to listen . . . listen to your breath and know God. Listen to your heartbeat and tap its rhythm—the God-cadence of your life. Tap, hum, listen, give thanks. Amen.

Scripture Sharing

In the beginning, God created the heavens and the earth.

Now, the earth was formless and empty, darkness was over the surface of the deep . . .

Now, the earth was formless and empty; darkness was over the surface of the deep . . .

And the Spirit of God was hovering over the waters.

The Spirit of God was hovering over the deep. The Spirit of God was hovering over the darkness and chaos . . .

> *And the Spirit of God stretched out, long and full—*
> *and kissed the face of deep darkness . . .*

The Spirit of God spread out and kissed the face of deep darkness . . .

> *I would invite you to be still for a few moments and listen to your interior. What deep darkness, what chaos in you is God reaching out to kiss with the wonder of creation? Allow the power of the Most High to overshadow You, and sense within you the new thing God is bringing forth . . .*

(Continue silence for several minutes . . . break silence with some music appropriate to your setting. I like polyphonic masses)

And God said, Let there be . . .

> So, let us be.

Let There Be Light In Me

"In the beginning when God created the heavens and the earth, the earth was a formless void and darkness covered the face of the deep, while a wind from God swept over the face of the waters. Then God said, 'Let there be light'; and there was light."

—GENESIS 1:1–3 (NRSV)

Before I had form

    when my face was hidden in darkness

    when I was mired in shame

God was creating . . .

The Spirit of God blew

    and kissed my tear-stained cheeks.

The Voice of God did not boom

    across the expanses of time and space

    (as one might assume)

But whispered, let there be light

in your hands and your feet

in your eyes and your mind

Let there be light

In your spirit and your smile.

And the light of Christ shined deep in my heart.

There was light . . .

And it was good.

Wander In The Woods

"Doth not all nature around me praise God? If I were silent, I should be an exception to the universe. Doth not the thunder praise Him as it rolls like drums in the march of the God of armies? Do not the mountains praise Him when the woods upon their summits wave in adoration? Doth not the lightning write His name in letters of fire? Hath not the whole earth a voice? And shall I, can I, silent be?"

—CHARLES SPURGEON
(19TH CENTURY THEOLOGIAN)

Lord Byron wrote, 'There is pleasure in the pathless woods.' And with this, I agree. Not because I find beauty in the jewel-green setting or in the notion of the wild—the reckless abandon—which one finds when traveling without a path. While these things are both true, it is something greater that brings me pleasure in this most unusual place.

It is that, while I wander a pathless way, I am not alone—and the maker of the woods is present with me. In each oak and rock and moss and stream—in each creature which scurries or slinks or slithers or slides . . . the Divine Master of the Woods—the Divine

Maker of the Way surrounds me. Calling me into union with all that teams with life around me. Making The Way, The Truth, The Life real, present, and known . . . even as I wander.

Earth's Heart Chakra

As I look out the windows

At raindrops and snowflakes

    twisted and tucking in their intimate embrace

Mother Earth is ringing out

    Green

Green ground

Green trees—the walls of my containment

Green Mother Earth

    pouring out love

And I wonder if her heart is right

Has she been spinning

    too fast

    too hard

    too long

Has she given and given

    the depth of her love

    the goodness of her heart

    the essence of herself

Is she gasping

    grasping to hang on

        to pour out every last breath

Until we find deep in our hearts

    the peace to pour out

    healing love for our Mother

Second Spring

earth awakens
    stirring from her gentle slumber
green shoots and yellow flowers
    push out from within
the promise of spring

for long, we have waited
    with bated breath
    for her arrival
for long, we have doubted
    whether she would truly come

yet, as birds call forth the dawn
    and the forsythia dances in the wind
the people are not to be found
    —save the wild call of a lone child

tucked away

    in hope and fear

    as fevers rage and lungs gasp

the people have turned inside

to keep their distant vigil

and watch through windows

    praying for a second spring

Incarnation: You are God-Stuff

Mary's Yes

A quiet voice answers

    Yes

        The mother of God

Who are we?

As we add our voices to the choirs of ages,

Do we offer songs of gladness and joy?

Are our voices dissonant or in harmony with the melody of God's song?

As it rings out across time and space,

As we are invited to join this never-ending hymn

Let this carol flow freely from our hearts

That our Yes might rise and we might serve.

Untitled No. 1

Stardust, lifedust
 birthed from within
Consumed and consuming
 passionate fire
Growth and change
 scorched seed
Opening to newness
 truth—life.

Christmases

The smells of butter in the air

Ginger and cinnamon rising

Sugar dipped fingertips

And home

Traditions and expectations of Christmas

Missing loved ones

As loved ones gather

Popcorn garlands

Carols rising

The fire sparks and burns

Igniting a longing for

    another time

    another place

    another Christmas

And still Hope rises

As angel voices sing:

Peace on Earth!

    For each of us

I Am The Mama

It's like every time I get used to the new thing . . . every time I adjust and get comfortable with the next diagnosis or device . . . something more is looming, lurking, ready to take me again by surprise. I got used to the NF diagnosis, the shadows on the brain, the tumors on the spine. I got used to the ADHD diagnosis, the world of neurodiversity, and the leg braces. I got used to the doctors' appointments, the therapy sessions, the meetings. I got used to teachers not understanding, to districts not comprehending. I got used to my child being the smartest person in every room, the IQ tests, the questioning of adults, the lack of appropriate work and respect. But now here I stand. 10 specialists, 12 specialists—I lose count. Another referral, another test, another biopsy. Haven't they taken enough of my child? Tonight's pain is nothing new. I have faced it before. But how many times must I face it again? Why must I conform to this new normal? This deep, soul-crushing Mama Pain . . . But after the little ones go to sleep, I will cry. I will grieve, again. Then, I will sleep, and I will wake. Because I am the pulse of my family. Because I am the Mama.

Be Still And Rest

As the little ones sleep softly in the corner
And the infant silently nurses in my arms
I am reminded . . .
Be still and know I am God.

These words

Which call me to task

Which hold me accountable

Which remind me of my failure

Too often I find myself
Distracted
Busy
Chasing the high of fleeting perfection . . .

And the evidence lies all around me

Like blocks scattered across the floor

Like a half-eaten sandwich

Like the growing mountain of laundry . . .

And as I chase this notion, I ask
What is perfect anyway?

Besides love . . . Besides God

> And in these moments
>
> When night gathers close
>
> And my eyes grow heavy
>
> I feel myself drawn closer
>
> To the breast of God.

God, the Mother

Who holds me

At the end of a long day

Tired

Worn

And invites me to rest.

> To rest in my imperfections
>
> To rest in unconditional love
>
> To rest and know
>
> Even I am a child of God.

Present To God And One Another

One day in prayer I asked,

    Lord, how can I be present with you?

    For You are always present with me.

    You go before me, You follow after me.

    You are at my right and left hands.

    You are above me.

    You are below me.

    You are in my comings and my goings.

How, O Lord, might I be present with You?

And a voice whispered softly,

    Be present with those I have given you.

Wee Hours With A Little One

In the fleeting hours
    of early morning
    before the sun awakes
I find myself
    wrapped in darkness
    secure
This sleeping child
    clings to my breast
    snores rising gently from his mouth
    sounding like a little piggie
His hair falling softly from his eyes
And in this moment, there is nowhere I would rather be.

Do Not Be Afraid Little Flock

Little flock, tiny ones . . . do not be afraid.

Do not be afraid of wolves and storms.

Do not be afraid—for I am with you.

Do not be afraid to preach the gospel of justice.

Do not be afraid to speak of radical love and peace.

Do not be afraid—for I am with you.

Do not be afraid to be yourself,

to be vulnerable and soft

for this is where you draw your strength.

Do not be afraid of you!

I have not made you to be vicious like wolves.

I have not made you to be violent like storms.

I have made you—as you are—in my image

to speak truth

to love mercy

to build justice

for my people.

Birthing Women

Like a phoenix—wrapped in fire
    decay and birth, birth and decay
an endless cycle of women—womanhood
we are different—yet we are one
    connected across age, beauty, and place
by the hope and promise of life
    created within.

Who Will Take Care Of The Mothers

Who will take care of the Mothers
    Tending to the world as large
    And the world at small
    The whole wide world and the world at home
Tending
Caring
Nourishing
Nurturing

But who will take care of the Mothers
With children to dress
    And wash
    And feed
A busy rush to get everyone out
    The door
    To work
    To school
    To play
Before she puts on her brave face to command the world

She works all day
Bearing the weight of
    Deadlines

    Sexism

    Outright misogyny

    Customers' frustrations

    Colleagues' expectations
Crushing her spirit
    Her soul

Before she put on again that shining face
    For pickups
    And drop-off
    For homework and dinner
As comments swirl around her
From all sides
    She should be more dedicated to her work.
    She should spend more time with her children.
    She should really think about her partner.
    She should really take care of herself.

Who will take care of the Mothers
As they go about running the world
    Being kicked around
    Knocked down
    Trampled under the wheels of progress.
Encouraged to have it all
And ending up with nothing

Nobody Offered

nobody offered to do my dishes

    or make my meals

    or vacuum my floors

nobody offered to wash my laundry

    so much laundry

    even though no one seems to wear clothes

nobody offered to tuck the kids in

    or read a bedtime story

    or hold the baby for a nap

nobody offered to take the big kids outside

    or play Legos

    or draw

but everyone kept asking me

    to prioritize

    to care

    to tend

to do the work

    the classes

    the job

to be the mom

    the wife

    the pastor

    the student

    the teacher

    the . . . everything

everything except the one with a choice

I became the one without agency

    without time

    without grace

and nobody offered.

Passion: You are Fire-Stuff

A Love Letter To My Church: An Ash Wednesday Lament

Oh Church,

It is Ash Wednesday today—and we are one week removed from the fiasco that was General Conference 2019. One week of drama. One week of trauma. And today, we enter into the season of Lent. A season of sackcloth and ashes. (Has anything ever seemed so appropriate?)

But while we prepare for mourning, for repentance, I keep thinking about the transfiguration story from this past Sunday. I keep thinking about my colleagues' courage to stand and speak in the aftermath of St. Louis. But something still bothers me. Over and over I hear and read their words reminding us to experience the glory of Jesus, to remember the mountaintop experience, that while we are called into ministry in the struggles of the valley, we need to keep our eyes on Jesus. But rock bottom will teach you lessons those mountaintops never will. We are called to minister with the living and dying, the hungry and hurting—those who dwell in the valley of the shadow of death. And I think that asking us to focus on the wonders of the mountaintop come from a place of privilege. Peter, James, and John even experience the transfiguration from a place of privilege. What about the other 9 who continued to struggle, who kept facing the horrors of reality and the hardships of humanity.

By focusing on the mountaintop, we once again ignore the struggle of those who hurt the most. And in the last week, so many of our colleagues have done just that. Like Peter, they are over-whelmed by what they see around them. They try to do what is right. Build a tabernacle. Put up a rainbow filter on their Facebook profile. But they have lost sight of the broken and the hurting. The cloud of good intentions has blinded their actions. And those most marginalized, those most hurting are left below in the valley—almost forgotten in the power of the moment.

But this is our struggle. This is the problem. Because while our colleagues focus on Jesus, we are bleeding. We are weeping—we have been eviscerated in the public arena. And we are being ignored. We have no place to call home—no place to be safe. As a victim of domestic violence, I know what it is to not be safe at home—no matter what pastors, DSs, and bishops may say.

And they keep pointing back to Jesus. That's all I've heard for the past week. Jesus, Jesus, Jesus. Keep your eyes on Jesus. Focus on Jesus. If you look to Jesus it will all be okay. Well, let me tell you something Church, I am sick and tired of your self-righteousness and your righteous Jesus! I am so tired of your judgmental Jesus. I am so tired of the King of Kings and Lord of Lords. Jesus—the name above all names. Jesus—the poster boy of the patriarchy! Well Church, I am sick to death of your Jesus. I am tired of your using this same Jesus to pit people against each other; tired of this same Jesus—the white supremacist, the oppressor of women, the executioner of LGBTQ+. Well Church, let me tell you, you can keep your Precious Jesus. You can keep your obsession with the cross, with the sins of others, with your own salvation. Keep the damn cross and your Jesus.

But, as a United Methodist, as a queer clergywoman, as someone who has felt the pain and rejection of Your Jesus, let me keep the flame. Let me burn with rage. Let me burn with passion. Let me burn and rise from the ashes.

Prayer To The God Of The Patriarchy

Dear God of the Patriarchy,

I am so sorry for praying to you beyond the box in which you reside. I am sorry for not conforming to your understanding of what is righteous. I am sorry for loving your children whom you have cast aside—thrown away. I am sorry that your Church has such a small vision of you that there are those who dwell outside your image. O God of the Patriarchy forgive me for thinking we might be something more.

#sorrynotsorry

Thoughts On Disappointment

I am disappointed in all the things.
Systems and structures
    we were told would protect us,
        could protect us.
But it was lies-
    it *is* lies.
What truth can be gained,
    from institutions
    that oppress and exploit,
    that pillage resources and abuse the people?
They ask—What is Truth?
    and feign ignorance-
    when they pull the strings
    to manipulate the world
I am disappointed,
    in churches that dismiss women
        that abuse queerfolx
        that pretend salvation is theirs to dispense.

in higher education that pretends those without a degree
are stupid

    that money equals value

    that health and wellbeing can and should be sacrificed
    for the illusion of normalcy.

that people and all of creation is disposable.

I am disappointed . . . and done.

The God Of Purple Lamé

This weekend, I saw God as a Drag Queen—riding a horse! Right?!? Who knew? She looked fantastic—let me tell you. She had this big, teased, blonde wig and a purple lamé bodysuit—with long sleeves and fringe at the waist. And she had this matching pair of kinky boots. You know the kind—with the 8" platform and the 12 buckles up the front? They were amazing!

And she called me, 'Beloved, what are you doing here?' I turned my eyes and sheepishly shrugged. Then she took my face in her hands and looked me in the eyes. 'I know why you are here. You are my beloved. I made you—just the way you are. This is something to be celebrated—and your family, your community, my beloved kin-dom is gathered here at Pride. Be unapologetically authentic—because that's who I made you to be.'

Starting to feel a little braver, I asked, Lord . . . what are *you* doing here? 'As if you could keep me away! As if you could hide from me!' she said. 'My people are here—and so am I!' Wanting to accept this, but having a knack for opening my big mouth . . . I gestured to her costume and ask, but why are you here like this? And she replied, 'Gurrl . . . It's cuz I'm fabulous!' We both laughed. 'Remember what drag is all about. It is about making a statement. It is about calling attention to something that world would rather ignore. It's about being so over-the-top visible; they have to see you.'

And then she spoke these words to me . . .

'Outrageous circumstances demand outrageous courage!'

I will say it again . . .

'Outrageous circumstances demand outrageous courage.'

Outrageous injustice requires outrageous action. We are past the time to sit by quietly and ignore what is happening all around us. People are dying because they can't afford to go to the doctor [during a pandemic, no less], children are being kept in cages at our border, [Flint *still* doesn't have safe drinking water]. [Coronavirus has compounded the already stressed systems and structures across our nation. Communities are waking up to recognize and respond to racial injustice.] We find ourselves facing injustice, even within the church. Our history of sexism and racism, of segregation and oppression, is calling us to repent, even when we want to deny its existence. Our beloved queer siblings are fighting—not simply for the right to marry or the right to be ordained in our church—but for their assurance of love and safety and liberation which comes from Christ Jesus.

The circumstances we find ourselves facing are outrageous— we are indeed outraged. But, as the God of Purple Lamé blesses us with outrageous courage—let us be bold enough to act. Amen.

Queer Clergy Hiding

What is wrong with me?

Why can't I just be myself?

Why do they say these things-

    that tear down?

    that cut deep?

    that destroy?

What is it that is wrong with me?

Is it the way I love,

    that is so wrong?

Or is it my call,

    that is so wrong?

Why do I do this work   when it hurts so much?

        when the pain escalates?

        when the harm is . . .

    suffocating?

Is my passion for God's people enough?

Is my spark for compassion enough?

Am I . . . enough?

What is wrong with me?

with me?

Come Out, Lazarus

the silence and shame of the tomb . . .

    of the closet.

crippling pain—crushing guild—the weight of love.

if only I had—if only I hadn't (!)

the church lied—the church died.

    death is final and resurrection is a lie.

I hold this truth, I am this truth, I live this truth,

    I die . . . this truth.

And then the voice of Christ cries,

    Come out, Lazarus!

Give Me The Fire

If I can only keep one thing
    give me the fire.
Give me the fire and passion to dance-
    to twist and twirl
Give me the fire
    a flame ablaze
    hot and red and orange and blue
deep and burning—give me the fire.

Give me the fire
    the passion for God
    to grow ever more in love
    to be remade by Spirit-fire
Burn away those things that hide me.
    That I may burn brightly for you.

If I can have only one thing,
    Give me the fire.

Untitled No. 2

I ask myself how many times must I wake
 Filled with dread
 Sounds of violence and hate
 Running through my head
And I ask myself what have I done
 To deserve this hate, this fight
 When darkness surrounds
 And day is the night
And I scream out the names of
 My daughter and wife

Fuck Lord—do not take them from me

What must I fight and where must I stand
 To protect my loved ones across this land
And God sneers down from his lofty throne
 And poisons the rivers
 And poisons my bones

Yet from the ashes, I will rise

And I will look him in the eyes

And profess a God that is kinder, gentler, wiser

>Within the bonds

>Between us

And proclaim hope once again.

I Was Surprised

I was surprised to see God as a Crone today. Now, that says more about me than it does about God. Her appearance startled me, just for a moment, until I realized who she was. Granted, our society has taught us to devalue the Crone, her wisdom, her experience, and especially her beauty. They have taught us that she is feeble-minded, that she is weak, that her looks should make us uncomfortable. And for a moment, I feared when I looked upon the face of God. But then I saw her long, flowing hair, shining like silver glitter in the sunlight. I looked and saw her soft face, weathered with time, weathered with pain. And her eyes, slightly sunken, sparkling with wonder and excitement when she caught my eye.

Many times, now, I have encountered God and I am used to her delight, her snark, her glory. Yet, I had never seen her as the Crone before—the wise woman, the witch, the hag. Never before had I seen her bent with pain, and grief, and age. Nor had I seen her wrapped in layers of red robes and cloaks. Her image would have struck fear in the hearts of men. And yet, her heavy eyes looked upon me and smiled.

She brought the experience and wisdom of all the ages, of all the world with her as a gift for me. She brought the dazzling innocence of youth, the heaviness of pregnancy, the challenge of labor and birth, and the joys and sorrows of motherhood. She understood the difficulties of nursing the world at her breast, of teaching her children, and of standing back and watching them make their own mistakes. She brought the pain of letting go and the wisdom of growth, the promise of hope contained in the constant of change.

Then I asked her, "My God, with all these gifts, why do you look so grieved? Why is it that your clothes are stained the color of blood?" Her words for me were heartbreaking and true and she said, "Beloved, my little one, my clothes are stained with the blood of my children—those harmed in my name. I carry their pain upon me, it is my cross to bear. While some hurl my name as a spear, others cut quick with the broken glass from a mirror. This mirror was for self-reflection and yet, they did not like what they saw and so they broke it and used its shards to wound those around them. And as the blood of my children runs, so my robes become soaked. It is this pain that wearies me. It is this burden which hunches my shoulders and weighs my spirit."

As I sat in the presence of her pain, the presence of her glory, I became aware of a truth. A truth about God, a truth about life, a truth about self. I was surprised to see God as a Crone today. She came vulnerable and tired, a little bit broken—like me. She came in the image most likely to be rejected, most likely to be feared, most likely to be hated. She came in all her wildness. She no longer caring what anyone thought of her . . . if she ever had. She came with glitter in her hair, sparkles in her eyes, and love in her smile. She looked upon her beloved and welcomed me into her wildness—knowing that the journey before us is long. And her wildness is in the wilderness. And the wildness of the wilderness is wrapped up in God.

By Tears And Fire

I'm sad and I'm mad and I'm frustrated and I'm exhausted as hell. I am angry with God and myself and the universe and well, I will be extra angry at God again—just for good measure. The hardest part is, I'm not really angry at God. I wish I were angry at God—because God is big enough to handle it. But I'm not sure the Church is. And that's where my anger really lies. I'm not sure the church can handle the rage offering of a 30-something bisexual female pastor. I'm not sure the church can hold the volume of truth I spew as I condemn their injustice. This is not the Church of Christ, but the Church of Men. And I weep for the destruction that will soon befall it. For mere mortals and divine beings have misplaced their trust and will suffer the bitterness of its collapse.

And I grieve for myself. I yearn for security—for a place in the order—but no one will have me. My training and years wasted in service to the Church of Men—all the while prophesying the present and coming kin-dom of God. But . . . we are always being poured out. Always being made new. And God cannot and will not be deterred. Rather She will wait and rise from the smoldering ash heap. She will rise from the depths of hell—the hell made for her by the Church of Men.

And She will bring forth life once more. She will draw her children from the four corners. She will gather them under her wing. And with the tears of grief and longing, She will baptize them with Holy Compassion. She will bring healing to their broken spirits and quench their dry bones. She will grow large and empty herself—hollow herself, like a bowl, that she might hold with love the tender rage of her people. And they might see wisdom reflected back at them. So, they can have a vision of justice—and peace can dance and swirl like sacred smoke.

For God does not fear us. God does not fear our anger or our grief or our femaleness or our queerness. God does not fear the shadows of our souls. Breathe on me, Breath of God. Cover me with your holiness—that I too may be holy. Dispel my anger according to your purposes or let it burn deep and consume me—not for destruction but for warmth and light. May your holy flames ignite your desires for my life. And as my body languishes in the fire, may your Spirit call forth the next generations to dance in the square and call down destruction on those who would defile your name and your children.

Holy Water Flowing:
You are Spirit-Stuff

I Thought I Was The Problem

I thought I was the problem. I honestly thought that I was having a particularly challenging time managing my roles as seminarian, pastor, spouse, and mother of three. I thought, since I am prone to bouts of depression, that I was just struggling. I had recognized it. I sought out help. I had talked to my DS, my partner, my SPRC. I had let my children know, "Mommy is having a hard time right now." I have been taking active steps to use healthier coping mechanism to manage my stress, because I have a whole bunch of unhealthy coping mechanisms that I fight back regularly. And then, I looked around.

I started listening to what was being said and not said by my clergy sisters. My fellow clergy moms were talking about feeling overwhelmed. They were talking about the frustration of anti-intellectualism. They were talking about the sexism they have been facing. They were talking about how hard it has been to adapt to children being home from school since COVID-19 closed everything down. They were talking about the excruciating pain involved in the decisions to re-open churches for in-person worship . . . and the hatred associated with decisions to remain closed for the time being. And, in the last 2 weeks, these incredibly challenging conversations (that never seem to disappear) have been overshadowed by one particular issue: our children's return to school for the fall.

Parents everywhere are now having to make decisions for their children's education for the upcoming school year. There are lots of choices—and none of them are good. Federal, State, and District guidelines are being changed left and right, and some Districts have not yet released their particular plans for the fall . . . and how could they when the nature of the virus and its impact on our communities shifts every day. Right now, the choices seem to fall into three really broad and vague categories: regular school attendance, virtual school attendance, and homeschool. Regular school would, mostly, put staff and students in the building, in some cases on a rotating basis and in others just return to pre-COVID procedures. Some districts are working on virtual school. In some cases, virtual school will be used to fill out the rotation of students in the classroom and sometimes as the way school will be this year. Having had a taste of virtual schooling this spring, questions remain surrounding time commitment and the accessibility of a virtual schooling approach. What about places without regular reliable internet? What about families who do not have computer access at home? What about the other support services schools provide to children struggling with challenging domestic situations and food insecurity? The seemingly last option then is home education. While some families are called to this ministry/ educational choice, many families with dual earning parents are considering this for the first time. How do homeschooling families balance two working parents, multiple children's curriculum, and required record-keeping? Luckily for UMC clergy parents, we are decent record-keepers by default. But how do we meet our work responsibilities and those to our children and their education? What about clergy couples with small children at home?

This is the general conversation right now. How do we manage everything and, in good faith and an understanding of science, send our children into school buildings where they could be exposed to COVID and become sick? Among parents of medically dependent, medically fragile, or special needs children, the conversations shift a bit darker. We are asking, how will my children receive the services they need if they cannot go to school? How do I send my child to school knowing their medical situation puts them at increased risk of, not just catching COVID-19, but dying?

How do I send my other children to school, knowing they will carry home this virus that will kill their sibling?

Then, I look back. I look at how I was feeling frustrated, overwhelmed. I remember saying, over and over again, that I was drowning. I remember crying out for help and thinking that maybe I was just weak. And then I realized that the system is broken. Because it is not just me. It is my beautiful sister who struggles with developing an educational plan for her child recently diagnosed with a brain tumor. It is my beautiful sister who is divorced and works at the conference office and can't figure out how to balance all the things. Its my beautiful sister who has learned her state's homeschool laws and filled out all the forms and the school district is still rejecting her homeschool plan. The problem is not just a Bekah problem. The problem is not that I cannot manage my household, or my academics, or my church. The problem is that the system is stacked against clergywomen, and clergy moms in particular. The denomination does not value us. . .does not value our ministry. Why else would we be placed in parish settings rather than station appointments? Why else would we be flung to the far reaches of our districts and conferences? Why else would we be told by conference staff that it was our choice to have children, so we just have to figure it out?

So, while I advocate for myself and my sisters, while I call for increased mental health services as no cost to us, while I call for support for clergy families, this is not *our* problem. We are doing amazing, innovative, creative ministry. We are re-defining ministry in our local churches. We are bringing God's kin-dom in this place. If there are resources to be found, if there are resources to be distributed, they should be for those holding the power within the denominational structure. Our boots-on-the-ground clergywomen have risen and continue to rise to the occasion brought about by COVID-19, the poor leadership of our nation, and our denomination. We continue to bring the love of God to the people of God. It is beyond time for our conferences and our leadership to recognize our gifts. We are re-defining what it means to be a pastor. We are re-defining how ministry looks in every context. But the expectations that need to be evaluated are those of the establishment. We cannot continue to use outdated metrics for measuring the success of our churches and our clergy parents. This is a new thing that Isaiah talked about. Changing the way the conference thinks about our ministry would be a far more productive use of time and resources than burdening our clergy moms with another book to read, another study to lead, another digital event to attend. We are already doing more than our fair share.

Finally, the study we have all been waiting for was published. It speaks to COVID-19's impact of working moms. Working moms have had a significant decrease in billable working hours since everything started. Moms are finding themselves pushed to the point where the choose work or kids. This study looked at dual income, heterosexual couples where both partners have higher education degrees, which is many of our clergy families. I would be interested to see the statistics for families where the mother has a higher education degree, and the father does not. I would be surprised if those mothers were not still making the choice of kids over work. It would be an utter disgrace to lose a generation of prophetic voices due to clergy moms stepping back from ministry. It is imperative that the United Methodist Church, her conferences, bishops, and leaders encourage and support our clergy families and the ministries of our clergy moms. As a clergy mom, I can tell you that our greatest resource is one another. The connectional nature of our denomination has created a network of amazingly strong and gifted women in communion with one another. We will continue to uphold and support one another in this messy denomination, this messy world, but the Church needs to recognize its failure to clergy moms and clergy families everywhere.

The Mug

While on a training retreat, as part of my spiritual direction pro-
gram, our facilitator asked us to bring our favorite mug to session.
While I had been using it all weekend to hydrate, and by hydrate,
I mean drink excessive amounts of coffee, we were asked to bring
our mugs empty to this particular session.

"Take your empty mug in your hands," she said. "Feel its
weight. Peer within and notice its capacity. See the colors. Imagine
its growing warmth, as it's filled with a rich refreshing beverage.
Feel the warmth spreading into your hands, your heart, and your
spirit. Experience this prayer and the comfort and presence of God
when you hold this mug. Amen."

I cried out to God . . .

I am void and empty!

God replied,

Just like the mug you encountered before.

You are void and empty.

And I will hold you.

Twisting The Image Of God

We cannot let what the patriarchy defines as church override the natural tendencies of Spirit-moving and working. For then, we become oppressive and domineering for Christ. Christ—The Victor! Christ—the King! Christ—the (Over)Lord! When we ignore and brush aside the nuanced presence of the Holy Spirit, we allow our faith to be weaponized . . . a tool for conformity, a tool for violence, a tool for our own supremacy. <If we can keep the hierarchy in place, if we can keep the duality in place, if we can keep those not like us in place, then we can be like God—for we have made Him like us!> Ugh, how disgusting!

If we can project and market an image of God that is white, dominant, and male, then those things that are white, dominant, and male will be celebrated and normalized. They will be given authority, or they will assume it. And because they are "like God" because God is "like them" they do not sin (because Jesus did not sin). Then their actions become excusable, permissible, acceptable, and celebrated. When these behaviors are not rooted in love, in relation to the struggle of others, they become tyrannical . . . and by extension, so does God. It is no wonder people are falling out with the church. It has twisted God into a malicious, callous, demanding fuckboy, who will get his way at all costs, and he doesn't care who he must trample to remain in charge. The heartbreaking piece is that is not at all who God is. The church wonders why millennials are embracing other paths—because there they find a warm and nurturing expression of the divine. In a world where religion has beat them, abused them, silenced them, excluded them—they are still seeking a God who loves them.

A Call For Justice And Action

It seems like there are so many injustices screaming for our attention. How do we triage? How do we find space to care? In the presence of rising fascism, a public health disaster, the detention and abuse of men, women, and children in concentration camps, the lynching of black men, the assault and murder of indigenous women, the systemic destruction of trans and queer people . . . how do we find strength? How do we continue when the environment is being destroyed, when communities are being destroyed, when human beings . . . are being destroyed? In militant fashion, human beings are being erased.

So many times, I cry out to God. So many times, I am met with silence. And I cry out to God again and again . . . as if in a vacuum, as if praying into a wall. The sound of my voice echoes back to my ears . . . hollow and hallowed. But in this holy and unholy disappointment, I am met by the eyes of Christ bringing me back. My spirit is strengthened by the one who brings us together and I am renewed. At the end of my hope, I am met by those of you who tend to the holy flame of hope within your breast. Ah, Holy Church, you are so very good. And in those moments, you lend your flame to me, reigniting my heart, my passion, my hope. You hold my frame as I cry salty tears. You offer a shoulder, an Advil, a sacred moment of prayer. And in that space, when our hearts have joined together, when your compassion for me is my only survival, Beloved, you call me forth. To a place of compassionate listening, to a place of holy rest, to a place of loving action, to be together.

Beloved, in these days when we cannot put one foot in front of another, when the powers that be exploit and oppress our bodies and spirits, we have hope . . . if nothing else. We have one another to help us journey on this sacred road. We have been summoned, called forth from our despair to build a kin-dom of justice and peace, and to preach the good news. And even in these days, when the Church and the Empire have become bedmates in a play for power, when people are hungering and thirsting for justice, when the good news seems so far away, we are called to bring the love of Christ, to nourish and nurture community, to be led by Holy Spirit power, and to build a new world, sing a new song. We must engage in holy mischief now. We must be part of the holy resistance. To not be cogs in a machine of destruction, but to partner with God in creating something whole, beautiful, and new. Our faith demands that much of us. And the road ahead is long. And there will be moments of exhaustion. And we will want to give up more times than we care to admit. But this is the good sacred work we have been fashioned for. To act for justice, to offer love and mercy, and to walk humbly with God . . . even in this world.

Untitled No. 3

Why does it feel like I am writing my last confession? Why is the pain so great—the division so wide? Deep and Wide—there is a fountain flowing deep and wide, but the water has been poisoned. It is not the cool refreshment of living water. It is not the reviving spring of justice and love. No, it has been corrupted. The water flowing chokes out the life. And I am helpless to stop it. I must now comfort the people in their thirst. I must tend to them in their distress. And I must lead them to new water. May God empower me to strike the rock, that waters may flow cool and clean. But, as of yet, I wander in this disoriented madness and feel for that which is wet. May I stumble upon it before my Spirit wears out. May I help another to drink the waters of life once again. May we, the people of the wilderness, have hope . . .

Water No. 1

Parched. Thirsting. Thirsty . . .

Water—for drinking, for cleaning, for healing, for belonging . . .

Do we pervert, corrupt, destroy the integrity

    Of Water

    Water intended for ritual—for washing

        When it is consumed?

Or do we make our errors when we bathe,

    In waters we could use to give drink

    To those who thirst?

Where is our righteousness found?

    In our rules

        Or

            In the compassion of life?

Workings Of A Mind In Grief

I am shocked. Overcome by emotion. Overwhelmed. I read it, and yet I cannot believe it.

Today, the church made a mockery of my ministry. It made a mockery of ME! Today the church disrespected my mother and my grandmother, her mother, and her grandmother. Today, the church disrespected my daughter, my precious child . . . my baby. As I try to raise her in a world where she sees herself as valued and important, today the church ripped at my spirit and tore every last ounce of worth I carried inside. I am bleeding, I am broken, I am screaming as a mother who has lost her child . . . the child of innocence . . . the child within herself. Today I am broken and frightened and angry and afraid because I don't know who I am anymore. I don't know what my purpose is. I don't know who can love me . . . when the church no longer sees me as one of sacred worth. When the divine spark that dwells within me is snuffed out . . .

. . . .

Do you know that feeling when you have been slapped across the face? And yes, it hurts. It hurts like a bitch—the stinging—the eye watering. But the shame and embarrassment and humiliation—that's what hurts the worst . . . That's how I feel right now. That's what the church has done . . . to me.

. . . .

A Stinging Slap

The stinging slap

across the cheek of the clergywoman

echoes in a vacuum . . .

We stand in stunned silence-

    Dumbfounded and confused.

As history rings in our ears

the challenge of the patriarchy rising

    carrying with it the authority

        to continue the oppression-

        to continue to hold us down.

But we are Methodists! we cry . . .

    And they laugh at us.

As the tears stream down our face

    —we are sneered at . . . laughed at . . . derided . . .

Our worth has been denied.

But we are Methodists! we cry.

    And we recall the women throughout the ages
    who have shaped our faith.

The women in the pews beside us.

The women in the Sunday Schools to guide us.

The women in the choir to chide us . . .

But we are Methodists! we cry.

And the church has turned her back on us . . . again.

For our only crime is being women.

For the only protections offered will not be afforded to us.

The victims of violence

    at the hands of men . . .

The victims of violence

    in the name of God.

The Pastor's Dry Bones

Ezekiel 37:1–14; John 11:1–45

I am feeling . . . well, kind of sorry. I reused last year's worship service instead of preaching something new. Instead of preaching, *again*. I mean, I have been preaching for 7+ years in multiple pulpits every Sunday. I have been preaching to my computer screen for over a year now. I thought, maybe, I had at one point in the last year said something deep or wise or at least good enough that I could take a breather this week. You know, being a pastor and a parent and going to seminary all at the same time during a pandemic is kind of exhausting. So, after prayerful consideration, I cheated. I just couldn't bring myself to preach the platitudes of John 3:16. Not again. Not now. Not when the world is so grieved—so full of pain. God may have "so loved the world," but I don't have time for it. That kind of love seems hollow, superficial, and empty right now. I need something with a little more substance. For me, John 3:16 is the sort of promise that has been overused, taken out of context, cheapened by basketball games, NASCAR races, and county fairs. While the wisdom and beauty of the promise are there for those willing to plumb the depths, right now, they fall on the ear like a noisy gong or a clanging cymbal.

But dry bones and dead men do not hear. And, oh, do I find myself in *that* valley. Maybe, you do too. Maybe, you find yourself in the valley of the dry bones. Maybe, you find yourself asking, "can these dry bones live?" Maybe, you find your spirit parched, locked away inside the tomb—stumbling through the valley of

67

the shadow of death. Oh, can these dry bones live? But see, in Ezekiel's text, God asks the prophet if the dry bones can live and the prophet answers, "only you know." My, how the tables have turned. Instead, we cry out to God, demanding an answer to *our* query—God, can these dry bones live? God, it was you who called me to do this work. It was for you that I answered your call. Now, answer me! Can you make whole again my fragile and broken spirit? Can you breathe life anew in me? Can you, O God, restore me? Heal me? Resurrect the fire and passion within me, that I may speak words of justice and love? That I may bear witness to your glory? Oh God, can these dry bones live?

And we, as pastors and faith leaders, know that God can call forth the dry bones. We know that God can call forth Lazarus from the tomb. And yes, we know that God can call forth the spirit in us. But what we need to know is if God is going to! We want to know if God is going to do it *now*! We are tired. Tired of being dry bones. Tired of trying to pour from an empty cup. Tired of moving through life as though we were dead. We are tired of waiting for God's Spirit to call out to us, awakening and reviving us. For we've already started to stink. But before Jesus called out to Lazarus— before the miracle of resurrection, Jesus wept.

Jesus wept, and Jesus weeps still. Jesus weeps for us and with us. In an embodied and present form, the God of all Creation grieved. God grieved the death of Lazarus. Even though Jesus knew what he was going to do, he still wept. He grieved with Martha and Mary—with the disciples—and with God's own self. Tears ran from his eyes and down his cheeks and into his beard, like the oil anointing Aaron. Holy tears made manifest in the sacrament of grief . . . an offering, poured out for humanity.

And as we await our own resurrection, God weeps with us. For those we have lost, especially in the last year, and for the little deaths we die every day. Whether we struggle, or rattle, or just lay still, God's humanity—God's divinity pours out on us compassion. God's holy tears become a baptism through which our spirits find life once more. God's holy breath will call us to live again. Maybe, right now, your spirit lays fallow within your chest. Maybe you wonder if any of this really makes a difference—if it really even matters. Maybe, like me, you find yourself exhausted by the platitudes and easy faith—this thing that has sucked you dry—made you brittle, fragile, and hollow. Maybe, like Lazarus, you can no longer feel joy or pain or fear or purpose.

I invite you to remember, God's Holy Spirit calls forth life. From the chaos, from the dry bones, and even from the dead. When Lazarus lay dead in the tomb, God still stepped forward. Spirit still called to spirit and brought forth resurrection. I know it feels like resurrection is so far off, like death is all that is present, that there is no hope for the future. But the God of Love is at work, even now. The God of Love is grieving with you—and for you. The God of Love is calling to your soul, "Come out and live." Bear witness to the God of Love. Bear witness to the God *with* us. Bear witness to the God of life. Life, even in this dry valley. Life, even in the shadow of death. Life, even in this world. Amen.

Pneuma Moved

and pneuma moved
a collective breath in
    and out
a sigh
    of fear
    of relief
the world
    panting
        shallow sips of air
    in and out
    in and out
and pneuma moved
    in us
    around us
    until We became One

River Of Life

the spring of my life
    bubbles up from the core of creation
    from my mother and my mother's mother
    stretching to the beginnings of time
this water—these waters
    primordial and deep
    swell up—overflowing
this is the ground-spring
    my dwelling
    my home

tributaries meet this water of life
    causing chaos
    and branching forth again
    they leave
        yet the stream is ever-changed
        always changed
        by their meddling

seasons of poisoning

of pollution

of abuse

yet the grandmothers' song has brought my healing

the River springs from across the sea

and finds its rest near the water's edge

dancing on the lakeshore

to Spice Girls

Ace of Base

4 Non-Blondes

to Judy Chicago

to Eve Ensler

tomato sandwiches and chocolate chip cookies

at my grandmother's knee

lazy days in the shade of the Willow

rising up

protective and safe

laughter and sisterhood

frustration and making up

but always together

under the mothers' wing

under the grandmothers' eye

but streams creep in

and muddy the waters

causing chaos and confusion

grief and pain
how does the River flow
when its existence
its identity—are threatened
when it is almost swallowed up
consumed by another
how does the River flow
when it is threatened to be overtaken
or to dry up completely

but deep within
I hear the mothers' song
pouring out healing
wholeness
restoration
and the River flows again
over rocks and pebbles
not tripping but gliding
on the strength of the song
and the River seeks out
those that are life-giving
those women of strength
that pour of themselves
to help the River flow again
each giving a little
that She might roar

and the River remembered the stories of youth
    of men and God and ritual
and She went about marking time and days
and pondering the presence of God
and knowledge of God and Jesus
    stood as a dam to the Spirit's presence

and the River meandered and traveled
    another path
    many paths
    listening, dancing, eating, praying

and when Jesus first spoke
    it was the voice of a man
in the darkness
in the night
    Jesus spoke kind words in silence

but as the River listened
    the kind words and gentle tones
    took on a feminine quality again
and She recognized this Jesus was the mothers' song

and the River leaned in
    and took up the song for herself
    She sang loudly—sometimes
        and whispered
the River listened to the song

and met Spirit

    in all her beautiful glory

and Wisdom marked the days

the River rested when Spirit set the course

    and reveled in their intimate embrace

    being carried in her sweet arms

        kissed by her soft lips

and the times the River resisted

    attempted to forge ahead

    the sweet, loving Spirit would hold back

    the moment of frustration

        of loneliness would rise

    until the River again finds its bounds

when keeping the course the Spirit sets

    the River dances and thrives

She does not pick up other's trash

She keeps from taking on troubled waters

and the River flows on

    dancing to the mothers' song

    following the Spirit's course

    pouring out the gift of life

        little by little

        to those whose streams are running dry

like a River, whose beginning is found

    from the swelling of earth

    a stream, cascading down the mountainside

        as milk flows freely from a mother's breast

my life wells up

    to nourish and nurture

    to tend and carry

    to sing the song

        that will encourage others

that we might be healed

that we might know justice

that we might seek peace

that we might Love—even in this world.

Who Am I Now

I got thinking today about the stupid question that often gets asked of those discerning their call to ministry . . . "What biblical character do you most relate to and why?" Ugh!! 10 years ago, when I began this process, I said, "Jeremiah." In Jeremiah, chapter 1, God tells the prophet, "Do not say 'I am only a child' for you must go where I tell you to go, and you must tell them what I tell you to say. My words will be on your lips." Now, as a 22-year-old female pastor with a small child at home, I understood the fear of stepping into a space where I would be working with and leading men 2,3, and 4 times my age. I felt I was a child, yet I felt the conviction of God within me. You *must* go, God says. Not, it would be really great if you could, or it might be nice . . . You *must* go! And I did.

For 10 years, I have gone where God has called. I have spoken the words God has put in my heart and on my lips. Even when I didn't understand. Especially when I didn't understand. Even when those words convicted the hearts gathered in worship. Especially when the words convicted the hearts of God's people. And I never really demanded anything of God in return. I knew I would be provided for because I knew God is faithful.

But now, I reflect on 10 years of preaching—of prophecy, of fire. I reflect on encouragement, on community-building, on friendships. I reflect on the ways my faith has shifted and grown. It now has overstretched its neat and orderly box. What used to hold my faith lies crumpled and broken on the floor—like an old shoebox in the back of the closet. Except my shoebox is church.

And as a pastor, tasked to tend to the religious community in a particular location, that's pretty dangerous.

Today, I think back on that same old question, and I realize the gift of Wisdom has been with me all along. 10 years ago, I was Jeremiah—the young one called to preach a hard, hard truth (Jer 1:7). But today, again, I am still Jeremiah, no longer young—no longer naïve. I have been hardened some by working with and against religious people. Their inability to listen is what is most painful. I see the desolation around me—all this which could have been prevented—if only they had listened—if only they had heeded the warnings. But they have brought calamity upon themselves and upon the people. And while a remnant will remain, while God will be faithful, I find myself in ashes and dust. A charred and spent reduction of what I once was—of what God dreamed for me to be. I am Jeremiah now, only older, and wiser and more filled with pain. I am the Jeremiah of Lamentations, and I have been called to walk in darkness with those long dead.

The Church has become the rod of the Lord's wrath—and it has taken on a life of its own. "He has walled me in; He has weighed me down with chains" (Lam 3:7–8). The Church took on the role of domination and conquest. It dominated the good news of Jesus Christ and lost its soul.

And yet, Pneuma moved. Ruach stirs, even now. And God is not contained. Maybe, life and breath are still the hope and promise for those who remain in the Lord. Maybe new and beautiful things will be conceived and birthed in darkness. And maybe the painful cries, the prayerful sighs, lifted in horror, might still rise.

For God is still God . . . and somehow, I still believe this Truth . . . even in this world.

New Faith: You are Changed-Stuff

Death Weighs Heavy

We are all old now

       of varying years

       of differing times

But life has come

       weighing heavy

It has aged us all

There are few moments

       of youthful splendor

       of joyful exuberance

No—we all understand

       feel the gravity

          if we are paying attention

Death comes and snatches

    those waiting

    those expectant

    those surprised

  And we have all come to carry the presence of Death

    the knowledge of uncertainty

    at our breast—under our wing

For Dr. Good

The best I could do
    was nestle in
    to a sheltered spot
    and stop to pray

To light a light
    in the wind at all
    for clarity
    for peace

Against the wind
    I struggled
    I broke
    I all but surrendered

And once the flame was lit
    I offered my prayer
    and rode home

Manna Came Today

Manna came today.

It didn't come down from heaven

    like a gentle frost

But it was delivered

    By a lunch lady in a blue apron.

She brought it to the passenger-side window of my van.

She tucked it gently on the seat.

She offered a smile

    "Stay safe" was her benediction.

Then, we drove home on desolate streets

    to see the bounty in Enough.

Four ham and cheese sandwiches

Four pb+j uncrustables

Four apple juices and four yogurts

Two cheesesticks, Three muffins, and a donut.

Four apples, Two oranges, and one plastic container of finely diced peaches.

Oh, those peaches—

the kiss of the Divine, covered in foil.

And three children sat,

And gave thanks for the goodness, the sweetness of God.

A Close Walk With Night

Night whispers around us—among us

Silently screaming of death

In a world of anger, disappointment, grief

Fear wells up

Tears spill over

Discomfort wraps like a blanket—stifling, suffocating

And we continue this close walk with Night.

Grandma God

Come to the table and come to the water and be fed and bathed and tucked in for the night. You will find comfort foods and a hot soak pair well with a heavy quilt and socks. This is a place for you to come and rest . . . like your grandma's house. There is no judgement. You are simply welcome. Eat well. Drink deep. Soak in the love. And there are chocolate chip cookies before bed. Then snuggle in and let me carry your worries for a while. You, dear, just practice being, breathing deeply and slowly. And know that you are so completely loved.

At The Table

Come to the table,

    she said, she said,

As she welcomed us into her home

You will find at the table,

    she said, she said,

The blessing of harvest and bone

All will be fed

    At the table, she said,

For all of us long to eat

Come to the table,

    she said, she said,

And nourish the Self that you meet.

A Strange Encounter During A Meditation On John 21

The eyes of my Lord did pierce me

With an intimate intensity—I could not look away

And he watched me—And I watched him; with our eyes
always locked

Never giving more than a fleeting thought to anyone outside—
us—And I took my seat and I ate what he fed me

And I never lost sight of those eyes: with their deep intensity—
with their tender compassion

The eyes of a lover

And we sat on that beach and our gaze never wavered

And his face shifted

> A hundred

> thousand

> times . . .

yet those eyes remained

And he drew me to himself, and he kissed my forehead
(as God always does)

And my body rested in God's own arms

And the many faces of Jesus invited me to see

Look Beloved—see yourself—you are beautiful—you are loved

You see the world in a different way

I know

    I made you

You see the world in me

You see me in the world

You have been given vision and for this you see

You see me

And now I shall see the world through your eyes

And the world shall see me through your eyes

Take this gift of vision and sight

    And help them to see

To see me—in many ways—in many faces

And know that I AM with you

I love you

And again, God kissed the soft spot on my forehead and my throat

And I closed my eyes to hold on a moment longer.

www.ingramcontent.com/pod-product-compliance
Lightning Source LLC
Chambersburg PA
CBHW052150090426
42741CB00010B/2218